Understanding Leadership Competencies

Creating Tomorrow's Leaders Today

Patricia Guggenheimer
Mary Diana Szulx

A Crisp Fifty-Minute™ *Series Book*

This Fifty-Minute™ book is designed to be "read with a pencil." It is an excellent workbook for self-study as well as classroom learning. All material is copyright-protected and cannot be duplicated without permission from the publisher. *Therefore, be sure to order a copy for every training participant by contacting:*

1-800-442-7477 • 25 Thomson Place, Boston MA • www.courseilt.com

Understanding Leadership Competencies

Creating Tomorrow's Leaders Today

**Patricia Guggenheimer and
Mary Diana Szulc**

CREDITS:

Product Manager: **Debbie Woodbury**
Production Editor: **Genevieve McDermott**
Editor: **Amy Marks**
Production: **Barbara Atmore**
Production Artists: **Nicole Phillips, Rich Lehl, and Betty Hopkins**
Manufacturing: **Stephanie Porreca**
Typesetting: **ExecuStaff**

For more information contact:

NETg
25 Thomson Place
Boston, MA 02210

Or find us on the Web at **www.courseilt.com**

For permission to use material from this text or product, submit a request online at www.thomsonrights.com.

ISBN 10: 1-56052-497-9
ISBN 13: 978-1-56052-497-7
Library of Congress Catalog Card Number 98-70396
Printed in the United States
4 5 6 7 8 08 07 06

Learning Objectives For:

UNDERSTANDING LEADERSHIP COMPETENCIES

The objectives for *Understanding Leadership Competencies* are listed below. They have been developed to guide the user to the core issues covered in this book.

THE OBJECTIVES OF THIS BOOK ARE TO HELP THE USER:

1) Understand the process of determining leadership competencies

2) Explore personal qualities of leaders

3) Discover actions that competent leaders

ASSESSING PROGRESS

NETg has developed a Crisp Series **assessment** that covers the fundamental information presented in this book. A 25-item, multiple-choice and true/false questionnaire allows the reader to evaluate his or her comprehension of the subject matter. To download the assessment and answer key, go to www.courseilt.com and search on the book title, or call 1-800-442-7477.

Assessments should not be used in any employee selection process.

ABOUT THE AUTHORS

Patricia Guggenheimer is the founder and president of Cavalier Development Company, Inc., an innovative consulting and training team. As an author, consultant, trainer, facilitator and national speaker, she has inspired leadership in banking, automotive, education, government, health care, information technology, national foundations, non-profit groups and public schools.

Ms. Guggenheimer holds a bachelor's degree of individualized study specializing in personnel issues and the law, and a master's degree in organizational development. She is a faculty member of the Graduate School, USDA. She has a proven track record of inspiring leadership in executives through one-one-one intensive coaching.

Mary Diana Szulc is the founder and president of MDS Consulting Group, Inc., a firm that develops leadership and management strategies and delivers seminars on areas that impact productivity, performance and profitability in Fortune 1500 companies. In her fourteen years at Xerox Corporation, Mary Diana held key management positions at line, staff and headquarters and played an integral role in developing and delivering the world renowned two week Xerox Manager School.

Ms. Szulc earned a bachelor of science degree with honors from Northern Illinois University in marketing and human resources management. She is a frequent lecturer and seminar leader for the University of Maryland system and the American Press Institute. Throughout her career, Mary Diana has presented to thousands of people in corporations, education, government and non-profit organizations encouraging individuals to achieve their goals.

PREFACE

Much has been written about change and the turbulence that ensues from organizational decisions to move in a different direction. Whether responding to a new competitive challenge, changing the focus of an entire department, or strategically planning a new change, we initially may respond with confusion, anxiety, or perhaps even excitement. We look for models that have worked, and we turn to leaders who can help guide us above the fray and do something about what is happening all around us. Leaders are more proactive, and they excel at bringing direction and challenge to the excitement of the change process.

Other topics receiving much attention include managerial competencies, both the basic skills and technical components, and various management theories that have given us many foundations on which to build our organization. These fundamentals of management theory and practice must already be in place in order to run an efficient organization. A more pressing concern is consideration of significant factors critical to good leadership.

In some cases, leaders emerge as the environment mandates. At other times, leaders shape their environment. In many situations, leaders sense their "leadership moment" and do what needs to be done. As such, leadership can be exercised by everyone on a daily basis when opportunities present themselves. Organizations need leaders at every level, but they need to practice leadership on a personal level, too.

Our goal is to help you achieve powerful results in your professional life as well as in your personal life. The exercises in this book help you create a road map to achieving self-awareness in nine leadership competencies. As you transform these exercises from paper to action in your life, you will bring a different leadership perspective to your professional, community, family, and civic responsibilities. You can then identify situations that need your unique leadership talents and abilities and make a difference in your day-to-day activities by acting in your "leadership moments."

"Excellent! A treasure chest full of refreshing ideas on leadership."

—MJ Cline, Manager, Employee
Development & Training, County of Henrico

"The authors offer a myriad of solutions to some of the most provocative challenges in the world of learning organizations. The reader will benefit from discovering key strategies to high impact leadership from these two consultants who have been there."

—Susan Zlatin, M.Ed., Director of Corporate Programs,
University of Maryland, Business School

"A good definition of brilliance is the ability to make the complex simple. Guggenheimer and Szulc do just that in 'Understanding Leadership Competencies': a novel, workbook approach to understanding what makes managers great."

—Vern Zelmer, VP of Worldwide Customer
Service, Xerox Corporation

CONTENTS

Dedications

To Scott D. Whitener, Ph.D., and James C. Fontana, Esq., who live and breathe all nine leadership competencies in their personal and professional lives—they are examples of the bridge connecting theory and practice. To my son, Matthew, a young leader whose impact will remain well after we are all gone.

—Pat Guggenheimer

To my mom, Helena, my greatest supporter, who has always encouraged me to follow my dreams. To my dad, Raymond, who has always wanted me to be the best that I can be. Thank you for being my parents. To Rev. Msgr. James W. McMurtrie, V.F., a spiritual leader who always makes time to give me advice on life when I need it most. To Andy Candreva, a leader who embraces these nine leadership competencies in every aspect of life.

—Mary Diana Szulc

ACKNOWLEDGMENTS

To the leaders who gave their personal time and energy to lay the foundation of this book, and especially to Ed Bersoff, Ph.D., Robert Buchanan, Ph.D., Barbara Flaherty, Susan Horne and John Ritzert, Esq. To Linda Couture for her continuous encouragement.

P A R T

I

Introduction

COMPETENCY: A DEFINITION

> *Competency: competence.*
>
> *Competence: Possession of required skill, knowledge, qualification, or capacity; having suitable or sufficient skill, knowledge, experience, etc., for some purpose.*
>
> —Webster's Encyclopedic Unabridged
> Dictionary of the English Language

All of a sudden, there is a global surge of interest in competencies. In the United States, the emphasis is on leadership competencies, driven by concerns about losing world-class status. As a concept, competencies have been around for hundreds of years. What differs today is the emphasis on choosing the competencies that will create wealth for organizations.

In the job world, *competency* has many meanings. Some definitions relate to the work—tasks, results and outputs. Others describe the characteristics of the people doing the work—knowledge, skills and attitudes (also values, orientations and commitments). A hybrid often mixes those two kinds of definitions and has been called an *attribute bundle,* a collection of knowledge, skills and attitudes. Attribute bundles use such terms as leadership, problem-solving and decision-making.

Competencies link organizational strategy with people, and people who are aligned with the strategic goals are better able to meet the challenges that global competitiveness requires. No matter which issues people face, they want to know where they fit in, what the work is, and what competencies they need. For organizations, it's a question of having the competencies to thrive. Competency-based approaches that go beyond past models and practices help address those issues. Competency response is a powerful answer to the problems people and organizations face in the next century.[1]

HOW THEY WERE CHOSEN

While most people in the leadership field are familiar with such competencies as problem solving, financial analysis, and marketing savvy, these skills do not, of themselves, make a leader. It is the nine competencies that make up the focus of this book, in addition to the traditionally valued competencies, which make a well-rounded leader.

From years of business experience, extensive research and observation, and interviews, and from the results of a focus group held in the United States, a competency model has been created that captures the essence of how leading people in a variety of industries and fields of endeavor have lived. Our research is based on leaders from corporate, private, government, community, and education sectors. Our purpose was to understand leadership competencies for the 21st century.

In our sessions, we gained agreement on the ground rules for the participants engaged in the study. We began with a "Behavioral Shopping Spree" to allow the participants to get to know each other and to start them thinking about leadership in behavioral terms.[2] The Behavioral Shopping Spree is based on the DiSC™ model of human behavior. Participants were given a list of behaviors and were asked to find as many other participants as possible who believed they exhibited those behaviors.

Once the participants felt more at ease with each other, we showed them the 67 core leadership competencies identified by Michael M. Lombardo and Robert W. Eichinger in the Career Architect® model. The facilitators read aloud the list of competencies, and terms were explained or clarified if needed. The list provided the springboard for the leaders to start thinking about the subject. It was used as a tool to help them describe the behaviors of successful leaders. Examples of the 67 competencies are

Action Oriented

Dealing with Ambiguity

Approachability

Patience

Business Acumen

Time Management

Caring About Subordinates

The facilitators next asked the participants to identify which competencies they thought were essential behaviors that a leader should exhibit. After considerable discussion as well as some modification and combining of terms, the group narrowed down the list from 67 to 9 competencies. The result is the identification of leadership competencies:

Passion

Humor

Courage

Integrity and Trust

Energy/Vitality/Enthusiasm

Building a Team

Setting Priorities

Creativity

Vision

THE LEADERSHIP CAPSTONE MODEL™

With the leadership competencies established, a model for leadership was built. The Leadership Capstone Model which follows is built on the pillars of management skills and financial acumen with the capstone consisting of the nine leadership competencies. There are many models that define management skills and behaviors as well as many courses on how to operate a financially efficient organization. By focusing on the nine leadership competencies of this model, you will have the framework to act in your leadership moments. Your personal mastery of the capstone piece will define and differentiate your role as a leader.

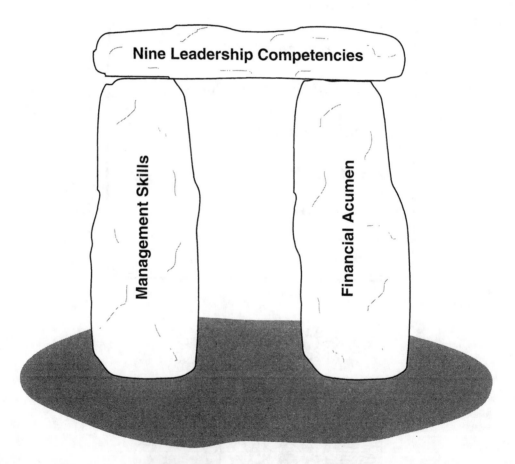

Leadership Capstone Model

CASE STUDY

A leader who immediately comes to mind as an exemplar of the power of our model is Aaron Feuerstein. Mr. Feuerstein owns the Malden Mills Textile factory in Hudson, New Hampshire. In December 1995, four buildings at the factory burned down, devastating the people of Lawrence, Massachusetts, many of whom were employees at Malden Mills. You can find this story on the Internet at CNN FN—The Financial Network, entitled, "CEO Bathed in Praise for Post-Fire Generosity." To recount briefly as of March 4, 1996:

Construction workers and heavy machines surround Malden Mills. They are busy rebuilding the four buildings destroyed and several others damaged in a debilitating December fire.

The experience was traumatic for everyone involved, but company president, Aaron Feuerstein, quickly stepped in to help his employees meet the challenges ahead. First and foremost among his goals was to ensure that their economic survival would not be threatened by the disaster.

Less than three months after the fire, 70% of the company's employees are now back at work. Production of polar-fleece fabric is expected to be back up to 90% of prefire levels by summer.

Just days after the fire, Feuerstein told all 3,000 of Malden Mills' employees that many of them would not be able to work until the destroyed buildings were rebuilt. Rather than sending them home without pay before the holidays, however, Feuerstein promised to give them full salary and health coverage for 90 days, a decision that could cost the company between $10 million and $20 million.

The decision carried a high price, but Feuerstein said the loyalty he won from his workers was priceless. "We're in operation today only because of the dedication of the workers. Once we made the decision, they did the balance," he said.

CASE STUDY (continued)

In spite of all the rewards from government leaders and religious and educational institutions, his colleagues in corporate America have yet to speak out in support of Feuerstein.

Professor Quinn Mills of the Harvard Business School said, "Many employers have probably been embarrassed by the way Feuerstein stepped in to help out." Feuerstein even honored Christmas bonuses that year.

The connection between Feuerstein's behavior and the leadership competencies in the Leadership Capstone Model is striking. His crowning achievement, or capstone, was living his leadership moment.

> While most business conscious managers would have been tempted to take the large sums of insurance money and fold up operations, Feuerstein cited a Jewish saying he learned as a child, "When everything is in moral chaos, try your hardest to be a 'mensch,' or man of highest principles."

Now you can see how important the Leadership Capstone Model is in terms of daily business life. Let's take a look at the high-impact results of Feuerstein's actions in terms of productivity. Three months after the blaze, the leadership dividend was indeed measurable—production had doubled since before the fire, and off-quality production had decreased from 7% to 2%.

You will hear about other individuals in this book who practice the Leadership Capstone Model. Feuerstein's leadership shows a highly developed self-awareness that can lead you to guide and direct with vision.

BUILDING YOUR CAPSTONE

The nine leadership competencies are the capstone every organization needs to develop for people at all levels. Our goal is to coach you as you build your own road map to developing these competencies. As a result of going through the exercises in this book you will:

- Become aware of opportunities to *act* in leadership moments.

- Become a risk taker and practice competencies you have not used.

- Incorporate competencies into your succession planning process.

- Grant people permission to act in *their* leadership moments.

- Build cohesive teams.

- Make a difference to your employees, peers, customers, and community.

- Provide a base to rebuild loyalty and trust that may have been eroded by downsizing and restructuring.

The nine leadership competencies build on traditional management skills of strategic planning, problem solving, decision making, delegating, and so forth. Therefore, mastery of both management and financial concepts is important to understanding the Leadership Capstone Model. With these pillars in place, you can begin to build the capstone of the leadership competencies.

My Key Learnings

Throughout this book we have carved out a section for "My Key Learnings" that is designed to assist you in jotting down your "ahas" from the section and/or competency completed as well as thoughts or actions you can start or stop doing immediately. You will be asked to review all of your Key Learnings and post the top three to five in the Summary of Key Learnings at the conclusion of the book. These Key Learnings will serve as your action list to plan future development. The next step is to decide upon which suggested interventions will help you reach your goals.

Take time to consider what you have just read. What have you learned about leadership competencies? What examples of these competencies have you noticed, in others or yourself? Make notes about any areas you would like to improve upon or would like to see others improve upon.

1. _____

_____

_____

_____

2. _____

_____

_____

_____

3. _____

_____

_____

_____

II

The Nine Leadership Competencies

INTEGRITY AND TRUST
BUILDING A TEAM
ENERGY · ENTHUSIASM ·
VITALITY   PASSION
SETTING   HUMOR
PRIORITIES   VISION
CREATIVITY   COURAGE

WHAT ARE THEY?

Now is the time for you to develop your own understanding of the nine leadership competencies. Through case studies and exercises, you will develop this understanding and assess your readiness to act in your own leadership moments. Each section also contains space to note your own key learnings and insights for action planning.

Our premise is that you need to know yourself and gain personal commitment to action through a thorough assessment of these competencies:

✔ **PASSION**

✔ **HUMOR**

✔ **COURAGE**

✔ **INTEGRITY AND TRUST**

✔ **ENERGY/VITALITY/ENTHUSIASM**

✔ **BUILDING A TEAM**

✔ **SETTING PRIORITIES**

✔ **CREATIVITY**

✔ **VISION**

PASSION

Passion: emotion; the emotions as distinguished from reason; intense, driving, or overmastering feeling or conviction; a strong liking or desire for or devotion to some activity, object, or concept; an emotion that is deeply stirring or ungovernable.

—Webster's Ninth New
Collegiate Dictionary

We have all been inspired by people like Bill Gates and Colin Powell because they are role models who continually strive against the odds to make their business objectives a reality. These are passionate individuals. The passions of Bill Gates are his work and the software industry. Colin Powell's passions are the future of children and his nation. One organization that exhibits passion is Rodel, Inc., a manufacturing concern based in Newark, Delaware. Rodel, a supplier of the electronics industry, manufactures polishing pads and slurries used to process silicon wafers and microchips.[3]

Eight years ago Rodel would have won no corporate-culture prizes. Internal strife was pervasive. Operating people didn't trust salespeople, mechanics nursed grudges against engineers, and department heads battled fiercely over budgets and turf.

"The place was a real meat grinder," recalls Dale Davis, a facilities manager, "an environment of intense emotion. If you could dominate a situation or grab the most resources, you were the winner." At roughly the same time, the company's owners, the Budingers, began to detect disappointment in some of their customers. Increasingly, the Budingers felt that without a fundamental change, Rodel would never achieve the quality, efficiency and cost-effectiveness necessary to compete long term against Asian companies.

The Budingers understood that uprooting ingrained work habits and implanting new ones would demand nothing short of a cultural revolution, a notoriously tough thing to manage. Therefore, to speed up the transformation, Leadership Intensive Training (LIT) was born.

LIT focused on teaching leadership skills. The formal regimen built around leadership underscored that Rodel's transformation was no fleeting fancy and was indicative of its long-term commitment. It was not another "flavor of the month." In fact, the LIT curriculum endures for a year, drawing from existing programs such as Outward Bound and from the writings of Stephen Covey and Peter Senge. Rodel thought a year would provide constant reinforcement.

On the premise that leadership could happen anywhere in Rodel, the program was open to employees from all departments and all levels. And remembering the grudging compliance of the supervisor's group, who chafed at mandatory attendance, they made the training voluntary. In fact, to add panache, they made it available by application only. To be considered, candidates first had to answer, in writing, five questions designed to weigh their commitment. The entrance exam was designed to gauge the depth of the employee's dedication to Rodel's success and their personal growth.

"Leadership Intensive, this whole way of working together, is a phenomenal competitive advantage for us," says Dale Davis. "It brings to bear the talents of everybody in making decisions and improvements. We're not the biggest company in our industry, but nobody else has this culture. We live, eat and breathe speed and response."

Bill Budinger doesn't pretend that the transformation is complete. There's no finish line. But LIT and other initiatives have kept Rodel in the game. "Otherwise," he says, "I doubt we'd still be here."

What inspired Bill to take this unconventional approach was, simply, his passion to succeed. More importantly, it was his passion not to fail.

EXERCISE: *Rodel Entrance Exam*

1. In what areas are you committed to growing in your leadership abilities?

   _____

   _____

   _____

2. One key to leadership is being a passionate advocate for something that forwards your (or your organization's) mission. What are you a passionate advocate for?

   _____

   _____

   _____

3. In your view, what is leadership?

   _____

   _____

   _____

4. What difference would your participation in a program similar to Rodel's make to you, your coworkers, and your organization?

   _____

   _____

   _____

5. What eventual responsibility or position do you see for yourself at your organization?

   _____

   _____

   _____

At the end of each competency section, you will be rating yourself on that competency. The results will be tallied in the Leadership Competency Grid at the conclusion of this book. The grid is designed as a visual representation of your strengths and weaknesses in the nine competencies.

COMPETENCY: Passion
Circle the number that represents your level of passion for leadership.
LOW   HIGH 0   1   2   3   4   5   6   7   8   9   10

Here are some practical suggestions for identifying and raising your passion competency:

- Take a leadership role in your organization by leading a committee.

- Tie in your community activities to your organization's mission statement and/or vision.

- Mentor an employee.

- Write an article on your passion for your company newsletter.

- Sponsor your company's sports team.

When you get involved in activities you really enjoy, you become energized and people can tell that you have a sense of purpose, which brings out your natural leadership abilities.

18

My Key Learnings

Take time to consider what you have just read. What have you learned about leadership competencies? What examples of these competencies have you noticed in others or yourself? Make notes about any areas you would like to improve upon or would like to see others improve upon.

1. _____

   _____

   _____

   _____

2. _____

   _____

   _____

   _____

3. _____

   _____

   _____

   _____

HUMOR

Humor: an often temporary state of mind imposed esp. by circumstances; . . . the mental faculty of discovering, expressing, or appreciating the ludicrous or absurdly incongruous.

—Webster's Ninth New Collegiate Dictionary

The use of humor by a leader helps to relieve day-to-day pressures and instill a feeling of camaraderie. Executives who are open with humor become more "human" and are more approachable to their employees. When people feel they can express their uniqueness, it allows everyone to see a different perspective and view things in a different light.

Living in our changing world involves uncertainty. "When John Glenn, the first U.S. astronaut in space, was asked what he had thought about just before taking off into space, he said: 'I looked around me and suddenly realized that everything had been built by the lowest bidder.' You can laugh, or you can cry."[4]

To some, humor is an illusion and is dependent entirely on the person who perceives it as such. There are different ways to be funny. There are the stand-up comics who are funny and make a living at it. There is the slapstick humor of the Keystone Cops and the Three Stooges. There is the infinite scheming of Lucille Ball.

In the everyday world, we all know people who are funny. We have a colleague named Rob Jolles who is quite the sales trainer. He uses a combination of stories, music, and props to get his messages across to the participants. He can use a certain tone of voice that invokes laughter as only he can. This is Rob's style, and it works for him. He uses humor to make learning more fun.

HUMOR (continued)

Rob says, "I believe when talking to a group of participants the real thrill is just how far you can push the humor envelope. Vincent van Gogh said, 'What would life be if we had no courage to attempt anything?'

"Humor is about risk. It is about taking chances. It is about doing something in front of a group that people may not find funny and working with it. What if they don't laugh? What if it is not perceived as funny? That, in a nutshell, is the risk. And that is where the challenge begins."

Other people crack jokes to be funny. Not all of us have the sense of timing to repeat a joke successfully. Yet we may have a dry or wry sense of humor. Some people play on words using puns. Others are humorous by poking fun at themselves.

What is humorous to you? Use the space below to list your favorite things that bring a smile to your face. Examples:

☞ Bugs Bunny

☞ Your favorite funny movie

☞ Your favorite comedian or performer

☞ _____

☞ _____

☞ _____

☞ _____

☞ _____

☞ _____

And sometimes we are just silly. The mundane becomes ridiculous. And sometimes seeing clowns gets us into the mood for humor. One of the easiest things to do to make someone smile is to put on a clown nose and smile.

List four ways that using humor as a leader works for you on the job. Some possible answers: *reduce stress and burnout, help others view a situation from a different perspective, release tension, reduce illness.*

1. _____

2. _____

3. _____

4. _____

Terry Paulson writes in *Making Humor Work: Take Your Job Seriously and Yourself Lightly,* "It is dangerous to confuse professionalism with seriousness. You can take your job and your world seriously, and still take yourself lightly.

"Human beings by nature are spontaneous and playful creatures. Yet the older we become, the less appropriate it seems for us to allow it to be expressed. We get 'professionally' serious and then pay comedians to do a job we've forgotten how to do ourselves."

One CEO expresses his humor very subtly. He wears the most professional attire and is immaculately groomed at all times. People comment on his beautiful ties regularly. Should you happen to sit across from him at a meeting, you would be pleasantly surprised to notice that Mickey Mouse and Donald Duck are woven into the fabric of a tie. What message is this gentleman sending? Perhaps that he is approachable, that he wants you to feel more at ease, take yourself less seriously, crack a smile, and also to relax upon meeting him.

What can you do to put other people at ease?

_____

_____

_____

EXERCISE: *Collage*

Another way to view humor is through creating a collage. The collage will give you a humor kick. Review the collage on a regular basis to remind yourself to use humor.[5]

Go to an art supply store and buy a piece of picture mat board and a glue stick. Pick your favorite color for the mat board. Then cut out pictures from magazines and newspapers that reflect you and what you find funny. You may choose anything that appeals to your sense of whimsy or is amusing to you.

Arrange the final selection of cut-out pictures on the mat board. Leave it overnight. The next day, see if you still like the arrangement—if not, change it. Then coat the backs of the pictures with the glue stick and press into place.

COMPETENCY: Humor

Circle the number that represents your level of humor.

LOW										HIGH
0	1	2	3	4	5	6	7	8	9	10

Nevertheless, some people just don't find anything humorous. We have a quote you should remember when these people pop up:

> *"Sometimes, no matter what we do, we get our heads cut off. And what goes around does come around."* [6]

You may feel that you are taking a risk in practicing some of the behaviors suggested. You will need to find your own comfort level with what works and what does not, based on the people you lead, the situation, the culture, the pressures of your industry, etc., but we invite you to work on incorporating this competency in some manner into your daily life. Studies have proven that you will live longer.

My Key Learnings

Take time to consider what you have just read. What have you learned about leadership competencies? What examples of these competencies have you noticed in others or yourself? Make notes about any areas you would like to improve upon or would like to see others improve upon.

1. _____
   _____
   _____
   _____

2. _____
   _____
   _____
   _____

3. _____
   _____
   _____
   _____

COURAGE

Courage: mental or moral strength to venture, persevere, and withstand danger, fear, or difficulty.

—Webster's Ninth New
Collegiate Dictionary

Sometimes people are imprecise about their desires, even to themselves. It takes courage to delve into your desires and to see what values are actually driving them. It may take a crisis to get you to face up to your fears and decide what really matters to you. The exercises in courage are designed to help you focus on your desires, where they come from, and what fears may be keeping you from attaining them.

CASE STUDY

There was a movement in Michigan to require subject matter competency tests for teachers in 1988. Scott Whitener, President/ CEO of the National Occupational Competency Testing Institute and former Dean of Education at Ferris State University, sat on a committee of deans representing fifteen public Michigan universities. All of the deans were opposed to competency testing except Scott, who thought it was a good idea. Scott was a strong advocate, and was responsible for developing the legislation. As a matter of fact, Scott was elected by his peers to chair the Dean's council and to serve as their chief spokesperson. In his opinion, "Teachers are not born, they are created. You have to know your content area. If you are going to teach history, you have to know history."

Although the other deans disagreed with Scott, they had great respect for him. He had the courage of his convictions to continue his advocacy for competency testing. In the face of opposition, with odds of 14 to 1, Scott continued to push for testing, eventually convincing the 14 deans of his argument's merit. He was appointed by the State Board of Education to oversee the process and implementation plan for competency testing. This process involved establishing standards and developing competency measures and tests as well as performance examinations. The result was implementation of the law that required teachers to be competency tested in the subject matter they taught. In Scott's words, the bottom line is: "You can disagree without being disagreeable. Stay the course." The biggest payoff is that the quality of public education in Michigan is improved.

Scott also believes people can live their personal lives courageously. Throughout his life, Scott has faced many adverse situations, yet he still has more vitality and energy than some people half his age. His most recent challenge is facing cancer for the second time. Yes, the cancer frightens him, but it does not stop him.

CASE STUDY (continued)

Scott demonstrates courage both personally and professionally. He believes in Stephen R. Covey's work and really lives this quote from *Principle-Centered Leadership:* "We need not be a victim of conditions or conditioning. We can write our own script, choose our course, and control our own destiny."

Scott has stated, "I don't mind that people know I have cancer. Some CEOs try to hide it because it is a negative. There is nothing to be gained by hiding anything. People can see me for who I am."

Scott says, "I believe it [cancer] won't get me. If you think you are going to die from it, you probably will. I see people who come every week for chemotherapy who don't have a good attitude, and they are not doing well. [If you don't think you are going to die, you won't.] The medical profession says it is 75% attitude and suggests you do whatever you have to do to keep well. You can't circle the wagons, and shoot at yourself.

"In a business situation this means that organizations circle the wagons, and conflict is turned internally. They try to protect their own territory and cannibalize. They end up with a confederacy instead of a union. They may trim unnecessary expenses, which makes the pie smaller. I prefer to increase sales and productivity and make the pie bigger."

Scott had the courage to stand up in opposition to all the deans. As a leader, what fears do you think he had to overcome?

_____

_____

_____

Name three people you think are courageous. What actions have they taken that exhibit courage? What other leadership competencies do they possess?

1. _____

_____

_____

2. _____

_____

_____

3. _____

_____

_____

Choose a situation you would like to influence. What fears will you have to face in order to achieve your goal? What actions will you take?

_____

_____

_____

The following exercise is an excerpt from Peter Senge's *The Fifth Discipline Fieldbook* and is quite useful here. The purpose is to describe your personal vision. Imagine achieving the results in your life that you deeply desire. What would they look like? What would they feel like? What words would you use to describe them? Use the present tense, as if it were happening right now. If the categories do not quite fit your needs, feel free to adjust them.

EXERCISE: Courage

SELF-IMAGE: If you could be exactly the kind of person you wanted, what would your qualities be?

_____

_____

_____

TANGIBLES: What material things would you like to own?

_____

_____

_____

HOME: What is your ideal living environment?

_____

_____

_____

HEALTH: What is your desire for health, fitness, athletics or anything to do with your body?

_____

_____

_____

RELATIONSHIPS: What types of relationships would you like to have with friends, family and others?

_____

_____

_____

WORK: What is your ideal professional or vocational situation? What impact would you like your efforts to have?

_____

_____

_____

PERSONAL PURSUITS: What would you like to achieve in the area of individual learning, travel, reading or other activities?

_____

_____

_____

COMMUNITY: What is your vision for the community or society you live in?

_____

_____

_____

LIFE PURPOSE: Imagine that your life has a unique purpose—fulfilled through what you do, your interrelationships and the way you live. Describe that purpose as another reflection of your aspirations.

_____

_____

_____

_____

_____

DEFINING COURAGE

If you're like most people, the choices you put down are a mixture of selfless and self-centered elements. People sometimes ask, "Is it all right to want to be covered in diamonds, or to own a luxury sports car?" Part of the purpose of this exercise is to suspend your judgment about what is "worth" desiring, and to ask instead: Which aspect of these visions is closest to your deepest desires? To find out, you expand and clarify each dimension of your vision. In this step, go back through the list of components of your personal vision that you have written down, including elements of your self-image, tangibles, home, health, relationships, work, personal pursuits, community, life purpose, and anything else.

Ask yourself the following questions about each element before going on to the next one:

If I could have it now, would I take it?

Some elements of your vision don't make it past this question. Others pass the test conditionally: "Yes, I want it, but only if . . ." Others pass and are clarified in the process.

You may, for instance, have written that you would like to own a castle. But if someone actually gave you a castle, with its difficulties of upkeep and its lack of modernization, your life might change for the worse. After imaging yourself responsible for a castle, would you still take it? Or would you amend your desire: "I want a grand living space, with a sense of remoteness and security, while having all the modern conveniences."

Assume I have it now. What does that bring me?

This question catapults you into a richer image of your vision, so you can see its underlying implications more clearly. For example, maybe you wrote down that you want a sports car. Why do you want it? What would it allow you to create? "I want it," you might say, "for the sense of freedom." But why do you want the sense of freedom?

The point is not to denigrate your vision thus far—it's fine to want a sports car—but to expand it. If the sense of freedom is truly important to you, what else could produce it? And if the sense of freedom is important because something else lies under that, how could you understand that deeper motivation more clearly? You might discover you want other forms of freedom, like that which comes from having a healthy figure or physique. And why, in turn, would you want a well-toned body?

To be more attractive? To play tennis better? Or just because . . . you want it for its own sake? All of those reasons are valid, if they're *your* reasons.

Defining all aspects of the vision takes time. It feels a bit like peeling back the layers of an onion, except that every layer remains valuable. You may never discard your desire to have a sports car, but keep trying to expand your understanding of what is important to you. At each layer, you ask, once again: If I could have it, would I take it? If I had it, what would it bring me?

This dialogue shows how someone handles this part of the exercise:

My goal, right now, is to boost my income.

What would that bring you?

I could buy a house in North Carolina.

And what would that bring you?

For one thing, it would bring me closer to my sister. She lives in Charlotte.

And what would that bring you?

A sense of home and connection.

Did you put down on your list that you wanted to have more of a sense of home and connection?

No, I didn't. I just now realized what is really behind my other desires.

And what would a sense of home and connection bring you?

A sense of satisfaction and fulfillment.

And what would that bring you?

I guess there's nothing else—I just want that. (Pause) I still do want a closer relationship with my sister. And I want the house. And, for that matter, the income. But the sense of fulfillment seems to be the source of what I'm striving for.

You may find that many components of your vision lead you to the same three or four primary goals. Each person has his own set of primary goals, sometimes buried so deeply that it's not uncommon to see people brought to tears when they become aware of them. To keep asking the question, "What would it bring me?" immerses you in a gently insistent structure that forces you to take the time to see what you deeply want.[7]

DEFINING COURAGE (continued)

Now, let's work on your vision. Ask yourself the following questions:

My goal, right now, is _____

What would your goal bring you? _____

And what would your answer bring you? _____

And what would your answer bring you? _____

And what would your answer bring you? _____

And what would your answer bring you? _____

Reflect on the answers you have given. What do you believe is keeping you from achieving your desires? Lack of money? Lack of education? Lack of time? What steps can you take to eliminate these obstacles and attain your desires? How does the leadership competency of courage relate to your achieving your goals?

_____

_____

_____

_____

_____

Name one courageous step you could take toward achieving one of your desires.

_____

_____

_____

_____

_____

COMPETENCY: Courage

Circle the number that represents your level of courage.

LOW   **HIGH**
0   1   2   3   4   5   6   7   8   9   10

Things you may want to consider to improve your courage quotient are:

- Call someone who is difficult for you to speak with, and suggest you have lunch together.

- Register for a continuing education course or workshop on something that you have been putting off learning.

- Provide support to someone who is not feeling well.

- Learn to coach a colleague on one aspect of his or her job.

- Choose a role model who exemplifies behaviors, values, and beliefs that show courage in action.

Courageous leaders fight their fears and do what needs to be done in the face of opposition. To quote Oliver Wendell Holmes, "What lies behind us and what lies before us are tiny matters compared to what lies within us."

My Key Learnings

Take time to consider what you have just read. What have you learned about leadership competencies? What examples of these competencies have you noticed in others or yourself? Make notes about any areas you would like to improve upon or would like to see others improve upon.

1. _____

_____

_____

_____

2. _____

_____

_____

_____

3. _____

_____

_____

_____

INTEGRITY AND TRUST

Integrity: firm adherence to a code of esp. moral or artistic values.

Trust: to rely on the truthfulness or accuracy of.

—Webster's Ninth New Collegiate Dictionary

What do you value? Integrity can be viewed as a set of values that we hold ourselves responsible for and demonstrate in our behavior toward others. We can develop and maintain integrity. We develop self-awareness and become independent thinkers by keeping our promises.

If we break our promises to ourselves and to other people, then we erode trust.

"Have you ever made a promise you didn't keep?" asked Clarence.

"Of course! Everyone, at one time or another, has had a good intention they didn't deliver on."

"What do you suppose happens when we don't deliver on something we've promised?" asked Clarence.

"Obviously, we lose trust and credibility. If it happens too many times, our promises become meaningless."

"That's what I think, too," said Clarence. "And that's why we have to walk the talk. Those good words you spoke earlier are like promises. People read and hear them, and then they expect the promises to be kept. But, if what they actually see is different than what they hear and read, there's a problem. Like my grandpa used to say, 'when you break a promise, more than the promise gets broken.' "[8]

EXERCISE: Integrity and Trust

The following exercise can help you look at your values. From the list below, check the top 10 values that are most important to you.[9]

Accountability	Efficiency	Privacy
Achievement	Environment	Professional Growth
Adaptable	Ethics	Public Service
Advancement	Excellence	Quality
Adventure	Excitement	Recognition
Aesthetics	Expertise	Religion
Affection	Friendships	Reputation
Affiliation	Geographic Work	Responsibility
Altruism	Home Environment	Security
Arts	Independence	Self-Development
Authority	Intellectual Stimulation	Self-Respect
Bonus	Life in the Fast Lane	Sophistication
Challenges	Location	Stability
Change and Variety	Loyalty	Status
Close Relationships	Nature	Tranquility
Community	Notoriety	Truth
Compensation	Open Communications	Variety
Competence	Passion	Wealth
Competition	Personal Growth	Wisdom
Cooperation	Physical Challenge	Work Fulfillment
Creativity	Pleasure	Work Under Pressure
Decisiveness	Portfolio Management	Work with Others
Democracy	Positive Attitude	
Effectiveness	Power	

Now narrow the list down to five (circle these). Next, cross off two of the five for a remainder of three. These three values are your most important ones. Write them here.

1. _____

2. _____

3. _____

Do you need to develop these values? ☐ Yes   ☐ No

If yes, how? _____

_____

Can you teach someone else these values? ☐ Yes   ☐ No

If yes, how? _____

_____

Once you have identified your core values, you may want to connect with organizations that have similar values. If you follow your values and passions, you will have balance in both your personal life and professional life.

REGAINING INTEGRITY AND TRUST

How do you demonstrate integrity and trust? Here is an example of a CEO of a midsize information technology company who is seated at the front of the meeting room. He has gathered each of the department executives that work for him to participate in a facilitated session to discuss a recent organizational assessment. The results point directly to problems with the way he is leading the group, so he is there to hear their complaints more directly and address how he will change.

At one point, one of his most senior and most valued employees asks plaintively, "What message do you think you are sending to us when you reschedule a performance review five times?"

What level of integrity and trust do you think the CEO has with this employee?

_____

_____

_____

How can the CEO regain his integrity and the employee's trust?

_____

_____

_____

COMPETENCY: Integrity and Trust

Circle the number that best represents how you exhibit integrity and trust.

LOW										HIGH
0	1	2	3	4	5	6	7	8	9	10

My Key Learnings

Take time to consider what you have just read. What have you learned about leadership competencies? What examples of these competencies have you noticed in others or yourself? Make notes about any areas you would like to improve upon or would like to see others improve upon.

1. _____

_____

_____

_____

2. _____

_____

_____

_____

3. _____

_____

_____

_____

ENERGY/VITALITY/ENTHUSIASM

Energy: the capacity of acting or being active . . . the capacity for doing work.

Vitality: power to live or grow.

Enthusiasm: strong excitement of feeling.

—Webster's Encyclopedic Unabridged Dictionary of the English Language

—Webster's Ninth New Collegiate Dictionary

People who have energy, vitality and enthusiasm are involved and pursue goals passionately. They put their hearts as well as their minds into their endeavors resulting in personal and professional fulfillment. These people tend to pursue many areas with equal abandon. They are driven to be the best at whatever they do, whether it is a hobby, a sports activity or a business transaction. These people have many professional and personal interests and are accomplished in many of these areas.

Personal vigor and the strength of a commitment to a vision creates a positive force that stirs employees to action. Once people are involved and action ensues, enthusiasm becomes contagious. Employees start to believe their own future goals can be realized through the organization's goals. By eliciting the cooperation of those in the organization by explaining the rationale or proposed activities, employees can visualize the steps necessary to accomplish results.

Our friend Kathleen has a great saying that "no grass grows under her feet." She is constantly on the go, energized by her passions and living her dream.

She is an entrepreneur who continues to innovate and develop others through her consulting work. She also reaches for personal mastery through her continuing education in a master's degree program. Kathleen is so involved with her passions that she excites others just by telling them what she is doing, what her next project is, and how she is going to approach her next marketing initiative.

We are responsible for maintaining our own energy levels. Papyrus stated, "No one keeps up his enthusiasm automatically. Enthusiasm must be nourished with new actions, new aspirations, new efforts, new vision. It is one's own fault if his enthusiasm is gone; he has failed to feed it." It is vital that we maintain both physical energy as well as mental vigor. One way to nurture your enthusiasm is to work through the following exercise.

EXERCISE: Energy/Vitality/Enthusiasm

Check off situations that energize, renew, and inspire you:

❑ Dinner conversation

❑ Coaching Little League

❑ Leadership training

❑ Self-development

❑ Going to the beach

❑ Talking with a friend

❑ Listening to music

❑ Project collaboration

❑ Volunteer work

❑ Team meeting

❑ Career counseling

❑ Curriculum development

❑ Acting in a play

❑ Vacation

❑ Celebrating your success

❑ Writing

❑ Getting a promotion

❑ Playing chess

❑ Mentoring process

❑ Problem solving

❑ Multicultural experiences

❑ Reading a book

❑ Going to the movies

❑ Buying flowers

❑ Visiting an art gallery

❑ Challenging work

❑ Using the computer

Choose your favorite situation and expand on it.

Situation: Talking with a friend

Reason(s): New ideas, support, fun, trusted listener

Situation: _____

_____

_____

_____

_____

Reason(s): _____

_____

_____

_____

CASE STUDY

Georgia Graves is an energetic, vital, and enthusiastic person. She is the president of a telecommunications company, president of the Greater Reston Chamber of Commerce, and drum major for the American Originals Fife and Drum Corps. She attends many committee and board meetings as well as many of the chamber functions in her various roles.

She also captures the essence of continuing the purposeful existence of Bridgman Communications. In this world of changing technological specifications in the telecommunications industry, Georgia realizes that she must set a strategic course for revitalizing her core business based on total upgrading of both mental capacity (learning new technologies) and physical products (changing equipment specifications).

It is essential that her employees continue their educational transformation by learning all the new technological advances that will be pivotal to moving forward in the 21st century. This learning has already begun with a plan to rotate staff through training courses while maintaining their present levels of customer satisfaction. Her commitment to employees' technical and career development showcases her leadership commitment to the vital principle of change.

Georgia attributes her leadership and business success to her company's major goal of "staying focused on keeping customers' telephone systems operating effectively. When problems occur, and you do have to plan on addressing problems, your enthusiasm level and good business sense will get you to the right resolution for the customer. It may be hard, and you have to do what is right. Doing wellness checks and preventive-maintenance checks with an optimistic attitude is key to maintaining the lifeblood [customer's telephone system] of the business. Always give 100% and always do the right thing. There is no other way."

COMPETENCY: Energy/Vitality/Enthusiasm

Circle the number that represents your level of energy/vitality/enthusiasm.

LOW										HIGH
0	1	2	3	4	5	6	7	8	9	10

A lack of this competency will result in falling short of your goals, even though you may have the opportunities. Good health is essential to leadership, so although you have heard it many times, let us stress the importance of taking good care of yourself. Henry S. Haskins stated, "Enthusiasm finds the opportunities and energy makes the most of them."

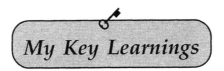

My Key Learnings

Take time to consider what you have just read. What have you learned about leadership competencies? What examples of these competencies have you noticed in others or yourself? Make notes about any areas you would like to improve upon or would like to see others improve upon.

1. _____
   _____
   _____
   _____

2. _____
   _____
   _____
   _____

3. _____
   _____
   _____
   _____

BUILDING A TEAM

Build: to develop according to a systematic plan, by a definite process, or on a particular base.

Team: a number of persons associated together in work or activity.

—Webster's Ninth New Collegiate Dictionary

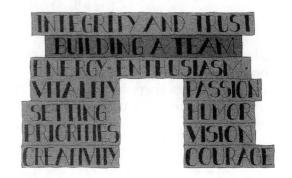

Books have examined the subject of teams from every perspective. Self-directed, cross-functional, office of the president, understanding the roles of team members, and so on. This section highlights the benefits of having a good working team by looking at how one *new* president/CEO used a strategic planning session to create synergy between herself and the existing team structure, which enabled her to establish credibility as their new leader. Judy Gray, President/CEO of the Fairfax County Chamber of Commerce, also wanted the team's input on creating a strategic plan that would be submitted to the board of directors prior to the start of the board's own strategic planning session.

Judy developed and distributed a questionnaire asking open-ended questions to generate objective input. It allowed her staff individually to gather their thoughts and data as well as to jot down any pertinent comments prior to the meeting. Then the team leaders met with their teams to collect all data and to come to a consensus on their priorities. This data was shared by each team leader at the main meeting. Judy was sensitive to the group dynamics because they would be discussing each other's work. She focused them on their tasks, roles, and responsibilities instead of on personalities. The questionnaire she used is shown on the following page. You can use this approach to building a team and building team commitment when you are a new leader of an organization.

EXERCISE: Building a Team

> **Strategic Planning Meeting Questionnaire**

1. What should be our strategy regarding competing organizations?

_____

_____

_____

2. What should we be doing more of?

_____

_____

_____

3. What are we good at?

_____

_____

_____

4. What do we need to improve? What should we offer that we do not offer now?

_____

_____

_____

5. Are there any activities/committees that we should restructure or just discontinue? Who will care? How do we know something is not working?

_____

_____

_____

EXERCISE (continued)

6. Is the staff organized in the best way? What alignments among jobs would make more sense? Who do you work with the most to get your job done?

_____

_____

_____

7. How can we operate even more as a team? Identify specific things we can work on.

_____

_____

_____

8. What do you need to be even more effective in your job?

_____

_____

_____

9. How do you measure the effectiveness of what you and others are working on?

_____

_____

_____

10. What would you change about your job if you could?

_____

_____

_____

TEAM BUILDING IN PROCESS

Judy Gray and an outside consultant discussed several meeting strategies to assure that the staff felt comfortable in sharing controversial viewpoints.

On the day of the strategic planning session, the consultant (who acted as the meeting facilitator) wrote the questions from the questionnaire onto flip chart pages to record the team's responses. The facilitator started to scribe, but as the meeting progressed, the participants assumed and shared that role. The established ground rules allowed for honesty of personal expression. Judy Gray commented, "People need permission to say the truth. The leader needs to be able to hear the truth." These are the ground rules to which the group agreed:

- "Don't waste my time (stay on topic)."

- All points of view are important.

- Honor the agenda—be on time from breaks.

- Acknowledge agreement of ideas, but avoid "violent agreement" as it is a time waster.

- Build on others' ideas to expand the concept.

- Allow the facilitator to determine the queue of people who want to speak.

The process entailed soliciting feedback for each posted question until all points of view were expressed. The room was wallpapered with participants' feedback, potential solutions to identified problem areas, and opportunities for new strategic direction. The decision was made to type the flip chart pages and use the resulting document as a guide to ensure continuity in strategic planning, goal setting, and implementation. Judy brought the meeting results to the senior staff, who determined what they could do immediately, what actions required board approval, and what they could not do.

These additional benefits resulted from the two levels of team building (i.e., at the board and staff levels):

- ► The staff realized they had authority to carry out many of their responsibilities without asking permission.

- ► The team helped the leaders identify issues of concern that the board needed to act upon.

TEAM BUILDING IN PROCESS (continued)

► The staff decided to

- Meet annually

- Tie objectives to year-end results

- Define what worked and what did not work

- Focus

- Tie the objectives for the bonus plan to monetary incentives and intangibles

- Celebrate successes

- Keep following the process rather than reinventing the wheel

► The board was informed in its long-term succession planning efforts.

► The executive committee meeting selected nine action items from the board and assigned responsibility for implementation to executive committee directors and their respective staff liaisons.

The immediate benefits of this session were:

✔ **Improved team morale**

✔ **"Real-life assessment" of the direction in which the organization was moving**

✔ **Better service to the organization's members**

✔ **A visionary, yet realistic strategic plan for the board of directors**

✔ **Encouragement of the team to grow toward becoming a learning organization**

COMPETENCY: Building a Team

Circle the number that represents your ability to build a team.

LOW										HIGH
0	1	2	3	4	5	6	7	8	9	10

As you can see, building teams helps organizations move to a competency-based structure. Team members know what skill sets are required and that their team members have these qualifications. Thus, mutual trust and respect are a foundation for team-based organizations. A lack of competencies tears down the infrastructure and is apparent in organizations that have lived through a mismanaged change. If you have been through a rough reorganization, you may want to focus on this leadership competency first, and then prioritize the remaining competencies based on what your teams need. Other interventions could include:

- Problem-solving and decision-making training

- Competency assessment and testing

- Facilitated team meetings

- An assessment mechanism

My Key Learnings

Take time to consider what you have just read. What have you learned about leadership competencies? What examples of these competencies have you noticed in others or yourself? Make notes about any areas you would like to improve upon or would like to see others improve upon.

1. _____
_____
_____
_____

2. _____
_____
_____
_____

3. _____
_____
_____
_____

SETTING PRIORITIES

Setting: the manner, position, or direction in which something is set.

Priority: a preferential rating; esp. one that allocates right to goods and services usually in limited supply.

—Webster's Ninth New Collegiate Dictionary

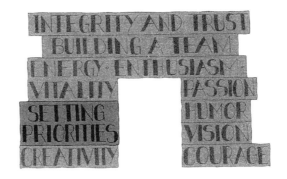

In today's busy world, it is difficult to set priorities. Setting priorities in your professional life is important and may affect your personal life. In an organization, there is a composite of people that each have their own personal priorities converging with the organization's priorities. Thus, in an organizational context, conflict can arise because people have different agendas. The way the organization handles these personal agendas determines the success of the enterprise.

"Setting priorities in an organization is an art. It is intangible. It involves thinking and in many cases, instinct. Priorities are fluid. They can change (and probably will) from week to week and often from minute to minute. It is like building a house, but the bricks are moving," says James Fontana, vice president and corporate counsel of Wang Government Services, Inc. Every organization will run into conflicting situations with government agencies, customers, or competitors. Suppose you are part of a multibillion-dollar organization that has been ordered by the government to clean up a toxic waste site. You have, in your opinion, met the environmental standards for disposing of the hazardous materials. You believe you have properly cleaned up the site and that the government is being overzealous and unfair. However, the next day, your organization is sued for noncompliance. The goal of the organization is not to lose, because you are right, and to minimize the damage to the organization's reputation. If you lose, you may have to pay severe penalties or, worse, declare bankruptcy, not to mention the enormous amount spent to defend your position.

SETTING PRIORITIES (continued)

Even if you win, you have to ask yourself whether draining your ogranization's resoures was worth it. The priority would be to prove the organization should be exonerated of all charges without destroying the organization in the process. The goal is not to win a battle at the expense of losing the war. Now it is clear that this goal will override all other goals. Depending on where an individual's priorities lie, the battle to establish them may become extremely personal. If personal values are closely aligned with an organization's values, then it's difficult to separate the line between personal and organizational priorities. Organizational priorities may hit you personally. If they are different, there may be conflict as to which priority is met first.

At this moment, what are your organization's priorities? What are your personal priorities? Do they align with one another? Complete the following exercise by addressing these questions.

EXERCISE: *Setting Priorities*

List the five most important organizational priorities you are challenged with:

1. _____

2. _____

3. _____

4. _____

5. _____

If you were transferred tomorrow, what would you miss the most?

_____

_____

_____

Do your organizational and personal priorities converge?

_____

_____

_____

Strategic priorities that are clearly linked to shared vision are instrumental in gaining commitment from the people in the organization. An individual or a team must be accountable for the priority so that achieving the priority becomes the driving force amidst the multitude of activities. You can measure or estimate whether you have achieved your priorities. These results will then enable you to determine what actions must be taken to achieve the vision.

COMPETENCY: Setting Priorities

Circle the number that represents your ability to set organizational priorities.

LOW										HIGH
0	1	2	3	4	5	6	7	8	9	10

EXERCISE (continued)

Which of the leadership competencies would help you address the organizational priorities that you have identified in this section? Solving critical business issues depends on your ability to incorporate the correct competency at the right time. Actions to consider:

- Reviewing your organization's mission statements

- Attending a work group development class

- Benchmarking best practices of other organizations

- Attending conferences and trade shows to learn industry trends

- Rotating cross-functional assignments

My Key Learnings

Take time to consider what you have just read. What have you learned about leadership competencies? What examples of these competencies have you noticed in others or yourself? Make notes about any areas you would like to improve upon or would like to see others improve upon.

1. _____
_____
_____
_____

2. _____
_____
_____
_____

3. _____
_____
_____
_____

CREATIVITY

Creativity: the quality of being creative; marked by the ability or power to create.

—*Webster's Ninth New Collegiate Dictionary*

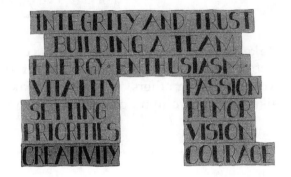

Some corporations foster creativity by constructing an environment that allows employees to unleash their talents while at the same time eliminating potential barriers. "Places don't create, people do," is an oft-said aphorism. While this is true, it is also true that a place can help or assist a person to be more creative.

CASE STUDY

Hallmark Cards built the Hallmark Innovation Center to foster creativity in innovation by providing a stimulating environment. The environment allowed different groups of employees to easily exchange ideas. The building is adjacent to the main Hallmark facility at corporate headquarters. It is accessible from the main building, but still, it is a separate structure.[10]

Creativity involves people talking together—sometimes in an office, sometimes in a lab, sometimes over a cup of coffee. Such creative brainstorming is what the Innovation Center is all about.

Collaboration is one key way to foster creativity. You may not have access to a separate creative facility; however, you can walk over to the next cubicle and discuss a concept with a coworker or colleague. You can call a friend or send an e-mail message. Through conversation and more structured techniques like brainstorming or *mind mapping* (see below), you can find solutions that may have appeared to be elusive.

Some people need 3D objects or blocks, some people doodle or draw, some people use the computer. Whatever your vehicle to stimulate creativity, you may find you are more creative than you originally thought. That creativity helps us to consider new alternatives and ultimately to progress in our professional and personal growth and development.

Sometimes we need to jump-start the creative process, by engaging our brain in a different thought process. Consider using mind mapping as a tool to stimulate creativity.

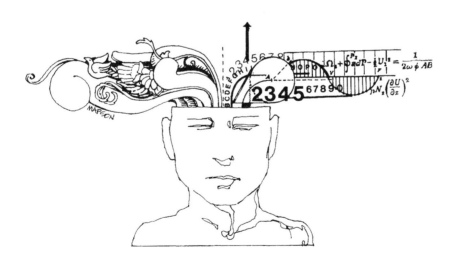

MIND MAPPING

The Mind Map is an expression of Radiant Thinking. Radiant Thinking refers to associative thought processes that proceed from or connect to a central point. It is a natural and virtually automatic way in which all human brains function. The Mind Map is your external expression of your own Radiant Thinking and gives you access to this vast thinking powerhouse. Mind Mapping is a powerful graphic technique that provides a key to unlocking the brain's potential. Every word and image becomes in itself a subcenter of association, the whole proceeding in a potentially infinite chain of branching patterns away from or toward the common center. The Mind Map can be applied to every aspect of life in which improved learning and clearer thinking will enhance human performance. The Mind Map has four essential characteristics:

1. The subject of attention is crystallized in a central image.

2. The main themes of the subject *radiate* from the central image as branches.

3. Branches constitute a key image or key word printed on an associated line. Topics of lesser importance are also represented as branches attached to higher-level branches.

4. The branches form a connected nodal structure.[11]

Mind maps help you to make a distinction between your mental storage *capacity*, which your Mind Map will help you demonstrate, and your mental storage *efficiency*, which your Mind Map will help you achieve. Storing data efficiently multiplies your capacity. It is like the difference between a well-packed or badly packed warehouse, or a library with or without an ordering system.

Here is an example of a Mind Map that depicts teamwork developed by Digital Equipment Corporation executives.[12]

The Group Mind Map

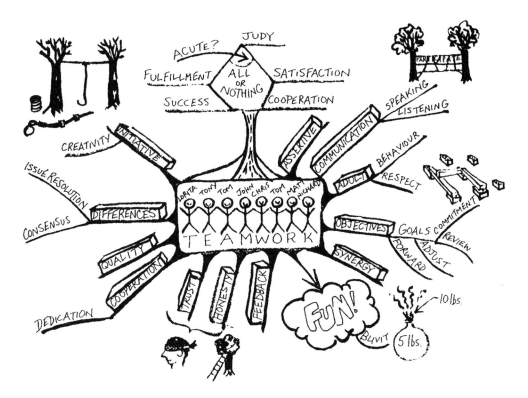

Mind Map on the development of team-work by Digital executives

EXERCISE: Creativity, with a Mind Map

Use the Mind Map Sketching Area below to mind map a central theme in your life. The theme could be work, family, or hobby. Write your central them in the oval and branch out from there. Let your mind flow.

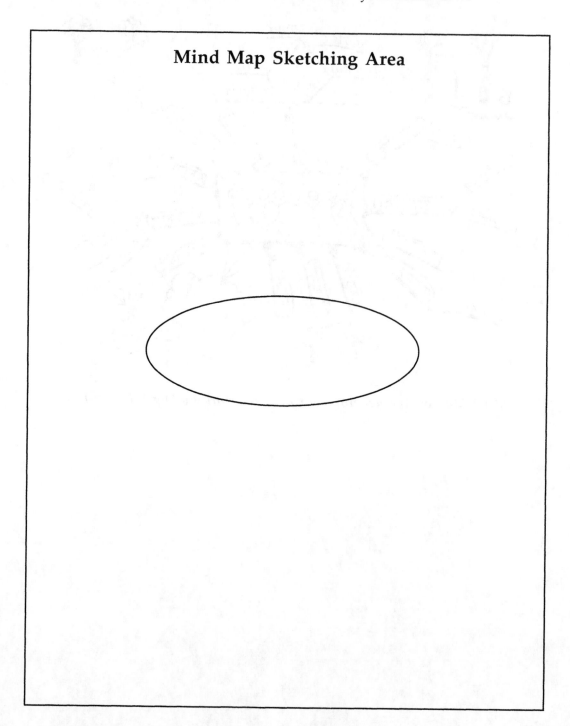

Mind Map Sketching Area

COMPETENCY: Creativity

Circle the number that represents your level of creativity.

LOW   HIGH
0   1   2   3   4   5   6   7   8   9   10

Other methods of creativity involve

- Brainstorming

- Utilizing a round-robin

- Playing games

- Working with a colleague

- Setting up an innovation center

- Going to an art museum for inspiration

- Calling your local library

- Holding think-tank sessions

Harnessing the collective talents of all members of your organization is critical to moving forward and maintaining a competitive advantage in today's global economy. By taking the time to instill in their employees that being creative is achievable and necessary, and by encouraging different forms of creativity, today's leaders are removing the traditional obstacles to releasing the creative expression of individuals.

64

My Key Learnings

Take time to consider what you have just read. What have you learned about leadership competencies? What examples of these competencies have you noticed in others or yourself? Make notes about any areas you would like to improve upon or would like to see others improve upon.

1. _____

_____

_____

_____

2. _____

_____

_____

_____

3. _____

_____

_____

_____

VISION

Vision: something seen in a dream, trance, or ecstasy; an object of imagination; the act or power of imagination; mode of seeing or conceiving; unusual discernment or foresight.

—*Webster's Ninth New Collegiate Dictionary*

We have concentrated on all the previous competencies so that you can assess your personal comfort level in each of them as a foundation for creating your vision. Without vision, there is little or no sense of purpose in an organization. Vision is building a personal commitment to values by creating visual images of the future.

Many books and other resources speak on vision. For example, Peter Block defines vision as, "Our deepest expression of what we want. It is the preferred future, a desirable state, an ideal state, an expression of optimism."[13]

It expresses the spiritual and idealistic side of our nature. It is a dream created in our waking hours of how we would like our lives to be.

Thus, an organization's vision should embody the collective values and aspirations of its individuals. The whole group should hold a "mental image" appealing to each individual's physical sense, emotional needs, and spirtual quests.[14]

Visions and intellectual strategies alone are insufficient to motivate and energize people at work. Sustained results come only if employees buy into a vision; they must believe that the leader's vision is their vision.[15]

CASE STUDY

Robert J. O'Neill Jr., the new Fairfax County, Virginia executive, is representative of building a vision and realizing the impact of building a vision. His story appears in an article published by the *Washington Post,* July 13, 1997. Robert was selected from a national field of applicants. As city manager of Hampton, he created a new vision for city government. The vision—to "become the most livable city in Virginia"—became a touchstone for city employees. It was even printed on their paycheck stubs.[16]

Following are some of the steps Robert took to help build his vision:

- An annual citizen-satisfaction bonus was given to every city worker.

- Each department had authority to develop awards for employee innovations and productivity improvements.

- Seed capital funds were allocated to test innovative ideas.

- Self-managed teams, multiple compensation plans, and Total Quality Management principles were applied.

- Statement of organizational values held managers accountable for their behavior.

- Venture teams went to other governments to find new ideas (competitive benchmarking).

- The city partnered with a neighborhood college to teach community groups how to participate in planning activities.

The result was that Robert swept away the bureaucratic culture of Hampton and replaced it with the organizational development enhancements above. In the hearts and minds of employees, bureaucratic culture was replaced by entrepreneurial culture.

Hampton received the Virginia Municipal League's Award for Entrepreneurial Government for 1993. Last year, Robert won a National Public Service Award from the American Society of Public Administration for "exceptional achievement."

The big payoff for Robert's career is that he is now recognized as a leader of an organization approximately six times the size of his former workplace.

Do you think that the employees understood and bought into the vision? Why or why not?

_____

_____

_____

_____

EXERCISE: Vision

Relating your story back to your workplace, you may want to consider the questions in the following exercise.

1. Do all the employees in your organization understand how vision relates directly to them? Cite three examples.

    A. _____

    B. _____

    C. _____

2. Sometimes a vision can be viewed as so far-reaching that individuals cannot see the connection between the big picture and themselves. Discuss among different departments how the vision directly affects them and actions to be taken.

Actions:

    A. _____

    B. _____

    C. _____

3. How about expanding this process further? Discuss how your organization's vision affects each employee on an individual level. Cite three examples, then dialogue and share answers.

    A. _____

    B. _____

    C. _____

4. As the leader of your group, list three to five ways you can communicate the organization's vision in your work group and across departments.

    A. _____

    B. _____

    C. _____

    D. _____

_____

COMPETENCY: Vision

Circle the number that represents your level of vision.

LOW										HIGH
0	1	2	3	4	5	6	7	8	9	10

DILBERT © United Feature Syndicate. Reprinted by Permission.

70

My Key Learnings

Take time to consider what you have just read. What have you learned about leadership competencies? What examples of these competencies have you noticed in others or yourself? Make notes about any areas you would like to improve upon or would like to see others improve upon.

1. _____

_____

_____

_____

2. _____

_____

_____

_____

3. _____

_____

_____

_____

P A R T

III

The Bottom Line

THE BOTTOM LINE

As we go through our day-to-day tasks, we rarely think of the competencies we use. It is important to look at our own work and acknowledge our strengths as well as what skills we need to improve. Your focus as a leader should be to lead your organization to success, however it is defined.

Here are three examples of situations where leadership competencies were exhibited to solve a problem. In each case, the organization has achieved positive results through the implementation of various competencies. Each organization has focused on a different aspect of its performance, and each has been successful.

(Focus on Employees)

Remember Aaron Feuerstein of Malden Mills Textiles? After the fire, his first goal was to ensure that the employees' economic survival would not be threatened by the disaster. Production has doubled since before the fire, and off-quality production has decreased from 7% to 2%.

What leadership competencies did Mr. Feuerstein show?

_____

How is a focus on employees exhibited in your own organization?

_____

(Focus on Competition)

Remember Rodel, Inc., and their LIT program? In the next several years following the implementation of this leadership, Rodel's sales grew by 50%. Their market share grew to nearly 40%.

What leadership competencies did Rodel's leaders show?

_____

How is a focus on competition exhibited in your own organization?

_____

THE BOTTOM LINE (continued)

Focus on Customers

Remember Robert J. O'Neill Jr.'s vision for city government? He wanted Hampton to become the most livable city in Virginia. He stressed "customer" (citizen) satisfaction in an entrepreneurial atmosphere where employees were allowed to come up with their own innovations and productivity improvements. Annual bonuses based on citizen-satisfaction were implemented.

What leadership competencies did Mr. O'Neill show?

_____

How is a focus on customers exhibited in your own organization?

_____

Think back to a problem you had difficulty solving. What leadership competencies could you have used to ameliorate the situation?

_____

_____

_____

Think back to a problem you solved using one or more of the nine leadership competencies. What actions did you take that demonstrated your skills?

_____

_____

_____

How did others respond to your leadership?

_____

_____

_____

P A R T

IV

Acknowledge Your Competencies

PUTTING IT ALL TOGETHER

Based on the situations you are facing every day, you can determine which of the competencies you will use to ensure the success of your efforts. This may mean that you will have to employ a different set of competencies than you usually do. Recognize that sometimes we have to "stretch" ourselves to make a positive difference in the lives of others. Since you have nine competencies to select from depending on the situation, the organization, the culture, the competition, and other factors important to you, you can take actions as required. Excellence is measured one step at a time, and it all begins with effort.

EXERCISE: *Putting It All Together*

Now go back through each competency section and transfer your rating to this Leadership Competency Grid. Then connect the asterisks for a visual diagram of your own personal leadership competencies grid.

Leadership Competency Grid

Competency	LOW										HIGH
	0	1	2	3	4	5	6	7	8	9	10
Passion	*	*	*	*	*	*	*	*	*	*	*
Humor	*	*	*	*	*	*	*	*	*	*	*
Courage	*	*	*	*	*	*	*	*	*	*	*
Integrity and Trust	*	*	*	*	*	*	*	*	*	*	*
Energy/Vitality/Enthusiasm	*	*	*	*	*	*	*	*	*	*	*
Building a Team	*	*	*	*	*	*	*	*	*	*	*
Setting Priorities	*	*	*	*	*	*	*	*	*	*	*
Creativity	*	*	*	*	*	*	*	*	*	*	*
Vision	*	*	*	*	*	*	*	*	*	*	*

Which three competencies do you believe have the greatest positive effects on your success in an organizational context? Why?

1. _____

2. _____

3. _____

Which three competencies do you believe have the greatest negative effects on your success in an organizational context? Why?

1. _____

2. _____

3. _____

Which three areas do you want to change the most? Why?

1. _____

2. _____

3. _____

Summary of Key Learnings

Review all of your key learnings and post the top five below. These key learnings will serve as your action list to plan further development.

1. _____
   _____

2. _____
   _____

3. _____
   _____

4. _____
   _____

5. _____
   _____

Leadership Competencies Matrix

The next step is to decide on your leadership goals, and the competencies that will help you reach them.

The Leadership Competencies Matrix which follows allows you to write in your own goals and decide which competencies are needed to achieve them. Now that you are aware of the areas in which you would like to improve, make an effort to do something about them on a daily basis. Share this leadership competency grid and key learnings with your colleagues, staff and other leaders.

Leadership Competencies Matrix

GOALS	Passion	Humor	Courage	Integrity and Trust	Energy/Vitality/ Enthusiasm	Building a Team	Setting Priorties	Creativity	Vision
Lead a committee	✔		✔			✔			✔
Serve on a community out-reach program	✔		✔	✔	✔			✔	
Mentor an employee		✔		✔	✔	✔	✔		

We trust you have found this book to be an excellent use of your time. If you would like more information on our Leadership seminars and workshops as well as our availability to speak to your group/conference, please contact us.

Carlson Learning Company facilitator kits, learning profiles, leadership instruments, and our Leadership Competency tool can be ordered from:

Patricia Guggenheimer
Cavalier Development Company, Inc.
Phone: (703) 392-1411 x309
Fax: (703) 392-8206
E-mail: cavdev@aol.com

Mary Diana Szulc
MDS Consulting Group, Inc.
Phone: (703) 729-5400
Fax: (703) 729-8977
E-mail: mdszulc@aol.com

We welcome your comments, feedback and success stories.

Endnotes and References

ENDNOTES

1. Adapted from Patricia A. McLagan's article, "Competencies: The Next Generation," Training and Development, May 1997. Reprinted from *Training & Development.* Copyright (May 1997), the American Society for Training and Development.

2. First published in the 1920s by William Moulton Marston in his book, *Emotions of Normal People,* K. Paul, Trench, Trubner and Co., Limited, England, 1928. Based on Marston's model, the *Personal Profile System®* was created and first published in 1972 by Carlson Learning Company. The value of the *Personal Profile System* is not so much that people learn how they view themselves and the environment, but that people learn about how they feel and behave in their unique situations. *Personal Profile System Facilitator's Kit* © Copyright 1996, Carlson Learning Company. "DiSC" and "Personal Profile System" are registered trademarks of Carlson Learning Company, Minneapolis, Minnesota.

3. Reprinted with permission, *Inc.* magazine, "Ready, Aim, Focus," Jay Finegan, March 1997. Copyright 1997 by Goldhirsh Group, Inc., 38 Commercial Wharf, Boston, MA 92110. (http://www.inc.com) Reproduced by permission of the publisher via Copyright Clearance Center, Inc.

4. Paulson, Terry, *Making Humor Work: Take Your Job Seriously and Yourself Lightly,* Crisp Publications, Inc., Menlo Park, California, 1989, p. 34.

5. Nancy Anderson, of *Work with Passion: How to do What You Love for a Living,* San Rafael, California, Copyright © 1984, revised 1995.

6. Harvey Eric, and Alexander Lucia, *Walk The Talk . . . And Get The Results You Want,* Copyright © 1995 Performance Publishing, Dallas, TX, p. 58. Reprinted with permission. 1 (800) 888-2811

7. From *The Fifth Discipline Fieldbook* by Peter Senge, Charlotte Roberts, et al. Copyright © 1994 by Peter M. Senge, Art Kleiner, Charlotte Roberts, Richard B. Ross and Bryan J. Smith. Used by permission of Doubleday, a division of Bantam Doubleday Dell Publishing Group, Inc., New York 1994, pp. 201–206.

8. Harvey and Lucia, *Walk the Talk, And Get the Results You Want,* p. 16.

ENDNOTES (continued)

9. Adapted from *The Fifth Discipline Fieldbook* by Peter Senge, Charlotte Roberts, et al. Copyright © 1994 by Peter M. Senge, Art Kleiner, Charlotte Roberts, Richard B. Ross and Bryan J. Smith. Used by permission of Doubleday, a division of Bantam Doubleday Dell Publishing Group, Inc., New York, 1994, p. 210.

10. Kuhn, Robert L., Editor in Chief, *Handbook for Creative and Innovative Managers*, McGraw-Hill, Inc., New York, 1988, pp. 271–272. Reproduced by permission of the McGraw-Hill companies.

11. From *The Mind Map Book* by Tony Buzan & Barry Buzan, New York, Copyright © 1993 by Tony Buzan & Barry Buzan. Used by permission of Dutton Signet, a division of Penguin Books USA Inc.

12. Buzan and Buzan, *The Mind Map Book*, p. 171.

13. Block, Peter, *The Empowered Manager*, Jossey-Bass, Inc., San Francisco, 1987, p. 103.

14. Reprinted with permission of Simon & Schuster Inc., from *Enlightened Leadership* by Ed Oakley and Doug Krug. Copyright © 1991 by Key to Renewal Inc., New York.

15. Manske, Jr., F. A., *Secrets of Effective Leadership: A Practical Guide to Success*, Leadership Education and Development, Inc., Columbia, TN, 1987.

16. Drawn from David Osborne and Peter Plastrik, 'The O'Neill Factor,' *The Washington Post Magazine*, Essex, MA, July 13, 1997, p. 8.

REFERENCES

Adams, Scott. *The Dilbert Principle: A Cubicle's-Eye View of Bosses, Meetings, Management Fads & Other Workplace Afflictions*, New York: United Media, Inc., 1996.

Anderson, Nancy, *Work with Passion: How to do What You Love for a Living*, San Rafael, California: New World Library, 1984, revised 1995.

Baker, Larry, Merrill Douglass, and Carlson Learning Company. *Time Mastery Profile.: Carlson Learning Company*, Minneapolis, Minnesota, 1992.

Block, Peter. *The Empowered Manager*, San Francisco, California: Jossey-Bass, Inc., 1987.

Briggs Myers, Isabel. *Introduction to Type*. 5th ed. Palo Alto, California: Consulting Psychologists Press, Inc., 1993.

Buzan, Tony, and Barry Buzan. *The Mind Map Book: How to Use Radiant Thinking to Maximize Your Brain's Untapped Potential*, New York: Dutton, 1993.

Carlson Learning Company. *Personal Profile System*. Vol. 3. Minneapolis, Minnesota: Carlson Learning Company, 1996.

Carlzon, Jan. *Moments of Truth*. Cambridge, Massachusetts: Ballinger Publishing Company, 1987.

Covey, Stephen R. *The 7 Habits of Highly Effective People: Powerful Lessons in Personal Change*. New York: Fireside, 1989.

———. *Principle-Centered Leadership*. New York: Summit Books, 1991.

Davis, Wynn. *The Best of Success*. Lombard, Illinois: Success stories—Great Quotations, Inc., 1987.

Finegan, Jay "Ready, Aim, Focus." *Inc.*, March 1997.

Harvey, Eric and Alexander Lucia. *Walk the Talk*. Dallas, Texas: Performance Publishing, 1993.

Kragness, Miriam, and Carlson Learning Company. *Dimensions of Leadership Profile*. Facilitator's Kit. Vol. 3. Minneapolis, Minnesota: Carlson Learning Company, 1994.

Lombardo, Michael M., and Robert W. Eichinger. *The Career Architect®*, Portfolio Sort Cards. Minneapolis: Lominger Limited, Inc., 1992, 1996.

REFERENCES (continued)

Manske, Jr., F. A., *Secrets of Effective Leadership: A Practical Guide to Success.* Columbia, Tennessee: Leadership Education and Development, Inc., 1987.

McLagan, Patricia A., "Competencies: The Next Generation," *Training and Development,* Alexandria, VA: The American Society for Training and Developing, May 1997.

Mirabile, Richard J. "Everthing You Wanted To Know About Competency Modeling." *Training and Developing.* Alexandria, Virginia: The American Society for Training and Development, August 1997.

Negroni, Christine. "CEO Bathed in Praise for Post-Fire Generosity." CNN FN—The Financial Network, the Internet, 4 March 1996.

Oakley, Ed and Doug Krug. *Enlightened Leadership: Getting to the Heart of Change,* New York: Fireside, 1991.

Osborne, David and Plastrick, Peter, (Drawn from) 'The O'Neill Factor.' *The Washington Post Magazine,* Essex, Massachusetts, 13 July 1997.

Paulson, Terry. *Making Humor Work: Take Your Job Seriously and Yourself Lightly.* Menlo Park, California: Crisp Publications, Inc., 1989.

Roberts, Wess. *Leadership Secrets of Attila the Hun.* New York: Warner Books, Inc., 1987.

Senge, Peter, Richard Ross, Bryan Smith, Charlotte Roberts, and Art Kleiner. *The Fifth Discipline Fieldbook.* New York: Doubleday, 1994.

Stazer, Ralph C., and James A. Belasco. *Flight of the Buffalo.* New York: Warner Books, 1993.

Swoboda, Frank. "Talking Management with Chairman Welch." *The Washington Post,* 23 March 1997, sec. H..

Szulc, Mary Diana. "Look for Leadership Moments," Greater Reston Chamber of Commerce Business Update, Reston, Virginia: The Times Community Newspapers, 25 September 1996, p. 6.

Webster's Encyclopedic Unabridged Dictionary of the English Language. dilithium Press, Ltd. and Gramercy Books, Avenel, New Jersey, 1989.

Webster's Ninth New Collegiate Dictionary. Merriam-Webster Inc., Publishers, Springfield, Massachusetts, 1984.

NOTES

NOTES

NOTES

NOTES

NOTES

NOTES

Now Available From

THOMSON
NETg

Books•Videos•CD-ROMs•Computer-Based Training Products

If you enjoyed this book, we have great news for you. There are over 200 books available in the ***Crisp Fifty-Minute™ Series***.
For more information contact

NETg
25 Thomson Place
Boston, MA 02210
1-800-442-7477
www.courseilt.com

Subject Areas Include:

Management
Human Resources
Communication Skills
Personal Development
Sales/Marketing
Finance
Coaching and Mentoring
Customer Service/Quality
Small Business and Entrepreneurship
Training
Life Planning
Writing